LET'S VOTE ON IT!

WRITTEN BY

CHRISTOPHER YEATES

COVER AND ILLUSTRATIONS BY

ZOE SADLER

© Gresham Books 2016
Published by Gresham Books Limited
The Carriage House, Ningwood Manor, Ningwood,
Isle of Wight PO30 4NJ
ISBN 978 0 946095 78 0

WHAT'S INSIDE

Democracy: what's the big idea? 4

The P word: Politics 6

How free are you? 8

It's all Greek to me: A brief history of democracy 11

Democracy in the UK 14

Democracy in action 16

Where it all happens: The Palace of Westminster 21

Political playground: The House of Commons 23

The main jobs of Parliament 26

The House of Lords 30

Do you remember? 32

BRITISH VALUES

Britain is made up of England, Wales and Scotland, and the people who live in these countries are called **British**. The people of Northern Ireland may also call themselves British and together we make up the **United Kingdom**. This book is to help you learn about and come to understand some of the British Values we all share.

DEMOCRACY: WHAT'S THE BIG IDEA?

Democracy is a big word and a big idea. The big idea is that in a democracy, a place is *ruled by the people*.

Being *democratic* is the name we give to the process of everyone having a vote or a say. Your vote gives you the chance to have your say and for your voice to be heard.

How democratic are you?

At school, your teacher will probably ask your class to vote on things that the class should decide together. For example, you will probably have been asked to vote for members of your school council. At home, perhaps each member of your family has a vote on where you go on holiday or what you have for supper.

The UK is a democracy. When you reach the age of 18, you are allowed to vote for the way you would like our country to be run.

The UK is a place where being democratic – and everyone having their say – is a very important idea.

What we mean when we say...

Democracy: a system where the people of a country vote for representatives to run the country.

Democratic: behaving in a way that supports a democracy.

Your turn to speak

Discuss with your partner why you think it is important that your voice is heard.

→ Can you think of anything that has happened at school because you voted for it?

Read and understand

1. In a democracy who has a voice?
2. What age do you have to be to vote for the way you would like our country to be run?
3. Design and draw a flag that represents the ideas of democracy – a place where the people have a voice and vote for representatives to lead their country.
4. What kind of choices do you have a say about at school or at home? For example, these might include being given a choice about what book you would like to read, or what you want to eat for dinner, or which film you want to watch. Give some examples of the choices you have a say about.

THE P WORD: POLITICS

Politics is the name we use to describe the activities of the people who run the country.

Every country in the world is run a little bit differently.

In Britain, the country is run as a democracy. In a democracy, all of the people have a voice in saying how the country is run. To help us organise our democracy, we have a *Parliament*, and we have a *Government*.

Parliament makes laws, decides how the country should spend its money and looks very carefully at the Government, to make sure the Government is doing its job properly. We will learn later about who sits in the Houses of Parliament to do these important jobs (see page 16).

Government is the group of people who actually govern, or run, the country. The Government is led by the Prime Minister.

HOUSES OF PARLIAMENT

What we mean when we say...

Politics: the activities of the people who run the country.

Parliament: makes laws for the country, agrees taxes and looks very carefully at the activities of the Government.

Government: the group of people that we have chosen to run our country.

Your turn to speak

Discuss with your partner:

→ Can you think of anything that you would like to raise with your school council? Perhaps you would like to suggest a change about what food you have at lunchtimes or even some rules at school. *Remember, if you don't use your voice, you will lose your chance to have your say about how your school should be run!*

→ Do you know anything about the British Government or the way it works? Do you know the name of the Prime Minister?

→ What do you think is the most important job of Parliament?

Read and understand

1. In Britain, we run the country using what kind of system?
2. Parliament has three main jobs – can you list them?
3. Design a poster showing what Parliament does.
4. Can you explain what politics means?
5. What is the difference between Parliament and Government?

HOW FREE ARE YOU?

Democracy depends on another very important idea; this is the idea of *freedom*. Being free means that you can act, speak and think however you like – as long as you are not hurting anybody else, and you do not break the law.

An important part of being free is having Human Rights. These are the rights – or freedoms – that every human should have.

Human Rights are about respecting each other, being fair to one another and understanding that everybody is as important as you are.

Some Human Rights you'll be glad to know you have:
➔ You have the right to be safe from harm.
➔ You have the right to follow any religion (or none).
➔ You have the right to speak freely.
➔ Nobody is allowed to make you their slave.

Human Rights try to make sure that everyone lives as happily and fairly as possible.

In the UK, our Human Rights should always be respected but, sadly, there are still many parts of the world where this is not the case.

What we mean when we say...

Law: rules we all agree to live by so that our society runs well. If a person breaks a law, they are likely to be punished.

Freedom: being able to act, speak and think as you please while still obeying the law.

Human Rights: privileges everybody should have because they are human.

Your turn to speak

Discuss in a group:

→ Can you think of some school rules that make life better for everyone?

→ Are there any school rules that you think are wrong and should be changed?

→ Do any members of your group follow a religion? Is it the same one? Share together some of the different ways group members follow their religion. Do you have special days for worship? Do you go to church, or a mosque or synagogue? Do you eat special food?

→ Discuss with your partner what you think would happen if we didn't have rules or laws.

Read and understand

1. Being free means that you can act, speak and think however you like – as long as you are not hurting anybody else, and you do not break the law. Design a 'being free' badge or symbol.

2. Who has Human Rights?

3. Look at the list of Human Rights on page 8. Which Human Right is most important to you? Can you explain why?

4. Why do you think we have Human Rights?

5. There are many more Human Rights than those listed on page 8. Do some of your own research to make a longer list of Human Rights that you can share with your class.

IT'S ALL GREEK TO ME: A BRIEF HISTORY OF DEMOCRACY

Democracy began around 2500 years ago in Ancient Greece, as a system for how great cities like Athens should be run.

The word 'demo-cracy' comes from two words in Ancient Greek meaning 'rule by the people'.

Every time an important decision had to be made, every free man in the city would gather together, discuss the issue, and vote on it.

Women, children, slaves and people not born in Athens were not citizens, and were not allowed to vote.

The Ancient Greeks' idea that lots of people sharing power is better than a few people telling everybody else what to do has become the world's main political system – democracy – but it isn't the only one.

Here are some other ways that countries have been run, or are run today:

→ **Monarchy:** rule by kings and queens.

→ **Dictatorship:** rule by a single individual.

→ **Communism:** everything is owned and run by the community.

→ **Oligarchy:** rule by a small group of powerful people.

→ **Theocracy:** rule by a religious authority.

→ **Anarchy:** where no one is in control and where any citizen can do whatever they like.

This is Andromeda.

She is an Ancient Athenian, and despite having some excellent ideas about how Athens should have been run, as a woman she would not have been allowed to vote and voice her opinions.

We have drawn her here to make sure you realise how lucky you are to be able to use your voice to stand up for the things that matter to you.

What we mean when we say...

Citizen: a legally-recognised member of a country, who has rights.

Vote: a formal way of expressing an opinion on something.

Your turn to speak

→ With your partner, discuss the different ways our country might be run if we didn't use democracy.

→ Pick one and imagine that the UK is being run using this system. Do you think this system would work better or worse than democracy? Can you explain why? For example, if Britain was run by a dictator, do you think this would be better or worse than a government voted for by the people?

Read and understand

1. Draw your own picture of Andromeda.
2. Where and when did democracy begin?
3. What does democracy mean in Ancient Greek?
4. Can you explain what a vote is?
5. Who was not allowed to vote in Ancient Athens?
6. Do you think Andromeda should have been allowed to vote in Ancient Athens? Give a reason for your answer.

DEMOCRACY IN THE UK

A monarchy is where a King or Queen is head of a country. Monarchs are not elected, which means they are not voted for by the people.

Many countries used to be ruled by an all-powerful King or Queen who made all the laws themselves. This type of monarchy was called absolute monarchy and was not democratic.

Today in Britain, we still have a monarch as our Head of State, but the monarch is only our symbolic leader and is not all-powerful. It is Parliament that actually makes our laws. This type of 'hands-off' monarchy is called constitutional monarchy.

Britain took its first steps towards democracy hundreds of years ago. For example, back in 1215, the barons – the richest and most powerful men in the land – made King John sign an important document called Magna Carta. This document said that the King had to obey the law.

It is only because people in the past used their voices to stand up for equality, that our Parliament today is truly democratic.

When you are 18 years old, you will be able to vote in elections, and use your voice to help decide how the country is run. It is very important that you use your vote.

What we mean when we say...

Absolute Monarch: a King or Queen who has unlimited political power.

Constitutional Monarch: a King or Queen who has very limited political power. The country is run by a democratic parliament.

Election: an organised choice that is decided by vote.

Equality: where everyone is treated the same and enjoys the same rights and opportunities.

Magna Carta: a formal document stating that the King had to follow the laws of the land. It guaranteed the rights of individuals against the wishes of the King.

Your turn to speak

→ Discuss with your talking partner what you think it would be like to be governed by an all-powerful monarch.

→ Why do you think the barons wanted King John to promise to obey the law and sign the Magna Carta? Make a list of reasons why you think the barons should have made the King sign this important document.

→ Do you think your school operates like a monarchy or a democracy? Explain why.

Read and understand

1. Picture the scene: draw your own picture of the barons making King John sign the Magna Carta.

2. Who is the Head of State in a monarchy?

3. What kind of monarchy do we have in the UK?

4. What is the difference between absolute monarchy and constitutional monarchy?

DEMOCRACY IN ACTION

So what is Parliament?

Parliament makes laws, and we call it the legislature.

The legislature is made up of three parts:
→   The House of Commons
→   The House of Lords
→   Our Constitutional Monarch

You can think of it like a jigsaw, with three pieces coming together to organise our democracy.

The biggest and most powerful piece of the jigsaw is the House of Commons, because that is the piece that the people have voted for in elections.

How does someone become an MP?

Every community in the UK elects one person to represent them in the House of Commons. This person is called an MP, or Member of Parliament. Each community is called a *constituency*, and there are 650 of them across the UK.

People vote for who they want to be their MP at least every five years on General Election day. On this day, everybody aged 18 and over can go to polling stations, set up across the country, to vote.

The candidate with the most votes in their constituency wins, and becomes the Member of Parliament for everybody in that community – even for the people who voted for someone else.

So what is the Government?

Most MPs belong to a political party. A political party is a group of people who have similar views on how the country should be run. When you vote for an MP, you are also voting for a political party.

The party with the most elected MPs in the House of Commons forms the Government, and their leader becomes the Prime Minister.

The Prime Minister is the head of the Government which runs the country. He or she lives at No. 10 Downing Street. The Government uses laws made by Parliament.

Both Parliament and the Government only have power because the people have given them power, which is why we call the system of government in the UK a *Parliamentary democracy*.

So what is a referendum? Ask the people!

Referendums are another valuable part of our democracy.

A referendum is when the people are asked their opinion on a single political question.

Giving each person a vote in a referendum means that everyone can have their say by casting their vote.

In June 2016, the British people voted in a referendum to decide whether Britain should leave the European Union. Many voted to stay in the European Union but even more voted to leave. The decision to leave, known as Brexit, was therefore a democratic decision.

What we mean when we say...

Legislature: another word for Parliament, which makes the country's laws. The legislature is made up of the House of Commons, the House of Lords and our Constitutional Monarch.

Parliamentary Democracy: a system in which people elect representatives to a Parliament to make laws.

General Election: when the country votes for the representatives who will become Members of Parliament. General elections happen at least every five years.

Constituency: one of 650 communities of voters within Britain which elect an MP to represent them in Parliament.

MP: Member of Parliament. MPs represent the views of the people in their constituency.

Political Party: a group of people who have similar views on how the country should be run.

Polling Station: a place where people in a community go to cast their vote in an election.

Referendum: a vote by the citizens of a country, on a single issue.

European Union: the European Union is a group of 28 countries who have agreed rules about how they live, work and trade together.

Your turn to speak

Discuss with your partner:

→ The House of Commons is made up of MPs voted for by the people. Why do you think this makes the House of Commons the most important part of the legislature? (Remember, the legislature is made up of the House of Commons, the House of Lords and our Constitutional Monarch.)

→ Which issues do you think the British people should be able to decide about in a referendum?

→ Are there any issues that you would like to vote on in a school referendum?

Read and understand

1. Draw a picture of the Prime Minister at home, at Number 10 Downing Street.

2. Make your own jigsaw showing the three parts that make up the legislature. In your picture make it clear which part is most important (the House of Commons).

3. What do MPs do?

4. How many constituencies are there in the UK?

5. Can you explain what happens during a General Election?

6. Time for some research... Do you know the name of your MP, and what political party they are a member of? It's really important to know all about your MP, because they represent you.

7. Is there an important issue in your community that you would like to write to your MP about, or perhaps an important campaign that you would like to support?

WHERE IT ALL HAPPENS: THE PALACE OF WESTMINSTER

The Houses of Parliament are in London, right beside the River Thames. They are made up of the House of Commons and the House of Lords. Their full title is the Palace of Westminster. The House of Commons and the House of Lords each have their own chamber, or hall. All of the seats and fabrics in the House of Commons are green and everything in the House of Lords is decorated in red, including the red leather benches that the Lords sit on.

The Houses of Parliament have over 1000 rooms, 100 staircases and three miles of winding passageways. Towering over the whole lot is the most famous clock tower in the world, and inside that a very famous bell: Big Ben. Big Ben chimes every hour throughout the day and weighs the same as a small elephant. A lot of people think Big Ben is the name of the tower or the clock, but it isn't – Big Ben is the name of the bell.

HOUSES OF PARLIAMENT

What we mean when we say...

The Houses of Parliament: the House of Commons and the House of Lords. They meet in separate chambers, and both are within the Palace of Westminster.

Big Ben: the nickname for the great bell of the clock at the north end of the Palace of Westminster.

Your turn to speak

→ Big Ben chimes every single hour of the day and night. If it is one o'clock, he chimes once. If it is two o'clock, he chimes twice. Working with your partner, can you work out how many times Big Ben chimes in 24 hours?

→ If you got the chance to interview your MP for a school magazine or newsletter, what questions would you like to ask him or her?

Read and understand

1. Where are the Houses of Parliament?

2. What is the full name of the Houses of Parliament?

3. What colour are the leather benches in the House of Commons? What colour are they in the House of Lords?

4. What is Big Ben?

5. Roughly how many rooms and staircases are there in the Palace of Westminster?

6. Make a fact sheet about the Palace of Westminster.

POLITICAL PLAYGROUND: THE HOUSE OF COMMONS

Most Members of Parliament belong to a political party, and the political party with the most MPs forms the Government which runs the country.

All the Members of Parliament from the political party which forms the Government sit on one side of the House of Commons chamber, and everyone else sits on the other side.

The Prime Minister and their ministers sit on the front bench. These important members of the Government are known as 'front benchers' and act as spokespeople for the Government.

The MPs from all the other political parties sit on the benches opposite the Government. The largest party are known as Her Majesty's Opposition, or the Opposition for short. The leader of the Opposition sits opposite the Prime Minister, and has a team

Government benches

Opposition benches

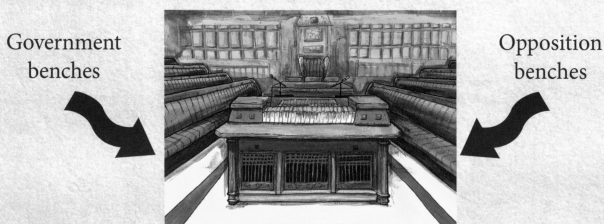

of 'Shadow Ministers' whose role is to ensure the Government ministers do their job properly. These members of the opposition are also known as front benchers. Can you guess why?

There are two red lines on the floor separating one side from the other, which were originally put there to prevent MPs from duelling and are just far enough apart that two drawn swords could not clash.

The Speaker of the House of Commons sits in the middle of the chamber between the two sides. It is the Speaker's job to keep the MPs' debates under control.

What we mean when we say...

The House of Commons: the democratically elected part of Parliament. It is made up of 650 MPs, one from each constituency. The House of Commons plays the most important role in creating and making laws.

Government: the group of people that we have chosen to lead our country.

Political Party: a group of people who have similar views on how the country should be run.

The Opposition: the MPs from the political party who have the second largest number of MPs. It is their job to challenge the Government on its decisions, and make sure the Government is doing its job properly.

The Speaker of the House of Commons: sits in the middle of the chamber and keeps everything under control.

Your turn to speak

Discuss with your partner:

→ If you were given the chance to ask your Headteacher about how they are running your school, what questions would you ask?

Read and understand

1. What is the leader of the Government called? Where does he or she sit?

2. Where does the Opposition sit?

3. Can you explain what the job of the Speaker of the House of Commons is?

4. Draw and label your own picture of the House of Commons, with MPs sitting on their green benches; with the Government on one side of the red lines and the Opposition on the other, and with the Speaker sitting and presiding over the chamber.

THE MAIN JOBS OF PARLIAMENT

MPs spend a great deal of time talking about issues important to our country. They debate about everything from housing to hospitals to what the Government is spending our money on.

Perhaps the most important debates are those discussing proposals for new laws. Before a proposal becomes a law, it is called a Bill.

Members of the House of Commons and the House of Lords try to improve a Bill by suggesting ways in which this potential new law might work better, or perhaps even pointing out why they think the potential new law might not work at all.

Then all the MPs vote on whether they think the Bill should become a law. If more MPs vote for the Bill to become law than those who don't, then the Bill has a *majority*. It has to have a majority in both Houses of Parliament.

Finally, the Bill becomes law when the Monarch gives it their approval; we call this getting Royal Assent. After a Bill gets its Royal Assent, the Bill becomes a new law, by Act of Parliament, and everyone in the country has to obey it.

The four main jobs of Parliament:

→ To pass laws and try to improve Bills before they become law.

→ To say how the Government should spend the country's money.

→ To make sure the Government is doing its job properly. This is called scrutiny. When you scrutinise something you are looking very carefully at it.

→ To discuss the many issues affecting the country, such as where our electricity and gas come from, or whether we should get involved in foreign conflicts.

Are you breaking the law?

A law is a rule that everyone in the country must obey. New laws are stored in a tower in the Houses of Parliament with thousands of other laws written on dusty scrolls.

Some of the older scrolls get a bit forgotten about, which means some very silly laws still exist. For example, if you've ever flown a kite in London you have broken the law. The Metropolitan Police Act of 1839 says so.

You will also have broken the law if you have ever had the plague and ridden in a taxi, or kept a pigsty outside your house.

You can also thank your lucky stars that you don't live in Oliver Cromwell's time, as he was so against people being greedy that he made it against the law to eat mince pies on Christmas Day!

But don't worry – there are hundreds of old laws that the police don't worry about any more!

What we mean when we say...

Majority Vote: the side that has more than half of the votes cast.

Bill: a potential law that has been suggested for discussion in Parliament.

Royal Assent: the formal approval by the Monarch that a Bill should become a law. A monarch hasn't refused to give their Royal Assent since 1707.

Act of Parliament: an action that creates a new law.

Scrutinise: to look at closely.

Your turn to speak

→ Make a list of the kind of topics that you think MPs discuss in the Houses of Parliament.

→ Discuss with your partner: Can you think of any new laws that you would like to introduce?

→ Look carefully at the four main jobs of the Houses of Parliament on page 27. Which job do you think is the most important? Can you explain why?

Read and understand

1. Make a poster showing the four main jobs of the Houses of Parliament.

2. What is the name given to a proposal for a new law?

3. Draw a picture of someone breaking one of the old forgotten laws.

4. Describe how Parliament makes a new law.

THE HOUSE OF LORDS

Unlike MPs, most members of the House of Lords are appointed rather than elected by voters.

Members of the House of Lords are known as peers. Peers, like MPs, look very carefully at Bills to see how these potential new laws might be improved.

There are three types of peer:
→ Firstly, you have peers who are appointed because of their special expertise in a particular area; these are called *life peers*.
→ The second type of peer are the 26 *Lords Spiritual*; these are the Archbishop of Canterbury, the Archbishop of York and the Bishops of the Church of England.
→ The final type of peer is a *hereditary peer*. Hereditary peers have inherited their position from their families. The vast majority of the House of Lords used to be hereditary peers; today, there are only 92. A male peer is called Lord and a female peer is called Lady or Baroness.

The Queen appoints new members of the House of Lords after the Prime Minister has suggested them to her. After a short ceremony, they join around 800 members of the House of Lords, who all help to craft great new laws to make the UK safer, happier and fairer.

What we mean when we say...

The House of Lords: the non-democratically elected part of Parliament. Around 800 Lords scrutinise and try to improve the Bills suggested by the House of Commons.

Life Peer: a Lord or Baroness who has not inherited their title. They are usually experts in a particular field.

Hereditary Peer: a Lord who has inherited their position from their family. Normally it is a Lord inheriting his title from his father, but some Ladies have inherited their titles too.

Lords Spiritual: the 26 bishops who sit in the House of Lords.

Your turn to speak

Discuss with your partner:

→ Think of some reasons why it might be a good idea to have a large range of experts looking at potential new laws.

Read and understand

1. Draw a picture of the peers sitting in the House of Lords. Remember the leather benches in the House of Lords are all red. Label your drawing with:

→ How many members of the House of Lords there are.

→ The three types of peer who sit in the House of Lords.

DO YOU REMEMBER?

Let's finish by reminding ourselves of some of the most important points we've learned:

→ Democracy first came into being in Ancient Greece over 2500 years ago. A democracy is a country ruled by the people. A democratic system is one where everyone has a voice or a say in how things are managed.

→ In Britain, the Government is elected by the people and is there to run the country, led by the Prime Minister.

→ Parliament is made up of the House of Lords and the House of Commons. Parliament makes laws, decides how money is spent and checks that the Government is running the country properly.

→ In Britain, our Human Rights are respected. Human Rights include the right to be safe from harm, the right to follow any religion (or none) and the right to speak freely.

→ A constitutional monarchy is one where the King or Queen acts as Head of State, but political power lies with an elected body such as a Parliament.

→ The legislature in Britain is made up of the House of Commons, the House of Lords and the constitutional Monarch.

→ At least every five years, we have a General Election to choose our MPs and our Government. Occasionally, we have a referendum to decide on a single issue that is important to everyone in the country.

It is very important that you use your vote!